SCIENTIFIC AMERICAN | EDUCATIONAL PUBLISHING

SCIENTIFIC AMERICAN INVESTIGATES FOSSILS

SEA CREATURE FOSSILS

BY NATALIE HUMPHREY

Published in 2025 by The Rosen Publishing Group
in association with Scientific American Educational Publishing
2544 Clinton Street, Buffalo NY 14224

Cataloging-in-Publication Data
Names: Humphrey, Natalie.
Title: Sea creature fossils / Natalie Humphrey.
Description: New York : Scientific American Educational Publishing, an imprint of Rosen Publishing, 2025. | Series: Scientific American investigates fossils | Includes glossary and index.
Identifiers: ISBN 9781725352100 (pbk.) | ISBN 9781725352117 (library bound) | ISBN 9781725352124 (ebook)
Subjects: LCSH: Fishes, Fossil–Juvenile literature.

Portions of this work were originally authored by Kathleen Connors and published as *Sea Creature Fossils*. All new material in this edition is authored by Natalie Humphrey.

Designer: Andrea Davison-Bartolotta
Editor: Natalie Humphrey

Photo credits: Cover, p. 1 (main) Tami Freed/Shutterstock.com; cover, p. 1 (vingette) Yurlick/Shutterstock.com; pp. 5 (top), 6 MarcelClemens/Shutterstock.com; p. 5 (bottom) Rebus_Productions/Shutterstock.com;p. 7 James St. John/Flickr.com; p. 9 (bottom) im.ismael/Shutterstock.com; p. 9 (top) Galyna Andrushko/Shutterstock.com; p. 11 Daderot/ File:Stromatolite, Proterozoic, Strelly Pool Formation, Pibara, Western Australia - Houston Museum of Natural Science - DSC01359.JPG/ Wikimedia Commons; p. 13 PRILL/Shutterstock.com; p. 15 (bottom) Catmando/Shutterstock.com; p. 15 (top) Marti Bug Catcher/Shutterstock.com; p. 16 Sponky/Shutterstock.com; p. 17 steve estvanik/Shutterstock.com; p. 19 frantic00/ Shutterstock.com; p. 20 lcrms/Shutterstock.com; p. 21 stihii/Shutterstock.com.

Printed in the United States of America

CPSIA compliance information: Batch #CWSA25. For Further Information contact Rosen Publishing at 1-800-237-9932.

Find us on 

CONTENTS

Words in the glossary appear in **bold** type the first time they are used in the text.

OCEAN FOSSILS

Paleontologists are scientists who study the ancient world by looking at fossils. Some of the most **abundant** fossils found on Earth are the fossils of ancient sea creatures. These sea animals may have been so small, they had only one cell. But some were larger than our largest living sharks.

By studying the fossils of sea creatures, scientists can learn more about life before any animal ever walked on land. Some of these important scientific fossil finds have even been made by kids!

FUN FACT
MARINE, OR OCEAN, PALEONTOLOGISTS ARE SCIENTISTS THAT STUDY THE ANCIENT OCEAN THROUGH FOSSILS.
Fossils are the marks or remains of plants and animals that formed over thousands or millions of years.

MAKING A FOSSIL

Many fossils are found in the ocean! This is because marine **environments** often offer the perfect conditions for fossilization. First, an animal or plant is buried in **sediment**. Sediment is usually found at the bottom of the ocean, rivers, and lakes.

Over time and under **pressure**, the sediment turns to rock. The soft organic, or living, matter of the plant or animal breaks down. This may lead to a fossil forming!

Some marine fossils, such as
this shrimp fossil, are thousands
of years old, but look like our
marine animals today.

DIFFERENT KINDS OF FOSSILS

Many marine fossils are the shell or hard **skeleton** of an ancient sea creature. Shells and skeletons leave fossils because they don't break down easily. **Permineralization** (puhr-mih-nuh-ruhl-ih-ZAY-shun) fossilizes some of these parts.

Other sea creatures left a kind of fossil called a mold. A mold forms when a sea creature's whole body breaks down, leaving behind an empty space in the shape of that creature. Sediment and minerals enter this space and create a fossil.

Permineralized fossils may show
more **detail** than other fossils.

FUN FACT

A FOSSIL MADE FROM THE
MINERALS AND SEDIMENT
THAT FILL A MOLD IS CALLED
A CAST FOSSIL.

MILLIONS OF YEARS AGO

Scientists have found fossils of sea creatures that lived over 3.5 billion years ago. These fossils come from tiny creatures called cyanobacteria.

Fossils show more familiar sea creatures starting to appear about 542 million years ago. This was during a period scientists call the Paleozoic era. Fish and jellyfish fossils date back about 500 million years. Scientists have learned from fossils that many marine reptiles first appeared about 299 to 251 million years ago.

FUN FACT

A REPTILE IS AN ANIMAL COVERED WITH SCALES OR PLATES THAT BREATHES AIR, HAS A BACKBONE, AND LAYS EGGS, SUCH AS A TURTLE OR A SNAKE.

TRILOBITES AND AMMONITES

The most common sea creature fossils are trilobites and ammonites. Trilobite fossils may date back 542 million years! These ancient **arthropods** had an exoskeleton, or hard outer covering, that was shed as the trilobite grew. The exoskeleton doesn't break down and many become fossils.

Ammonite fossils are curved and look a bit like seashells. They may be anywhere from 450 to 65 million years old. Ammonites lived in the ocean for a long period of time!

The largest trilobite was
28 inches (70 cm) long.

GIANT SEA CREATURES

Marine paleontologists have found more than just small sea creatures! Ancient reptiles that are related to today's reptiles have also been found.

Plesiosaurs were one kind of marine reptile that left behind many fossils. They lived in the Pacific Ocean and the seas of what is now Europe. They swam using wide, flat fins. Paleontologists have found fossils from two kinds of plesiosaurs: short-necked pliosaurs and long-necked plesiosauroids.

Some ancient plesiosaur fossils date back 215 to 80 million years.

FUN FACT

PLESIOSAURS LIVED AT THE SAME TIME AS MANY DINOSAURS, BUT THEY AREN'T DINOSAURS AT ALL! THIS MARINE REPTILE IS PART OF ITS OWN GROUP AND MANY OUTLIVED DINOSAURS.

15

INDEX FOSSILS

Index fossils are fossils scientists use to note certain time periods on Earth. These fossils are plentiful, found in many places, and lived only during certain periods.

Index fossils tell scientists when other fossilized creatures may have lived. For example, scientists know when different types of ammonites lived. If a fossil of one kind of ammonite is found in the same rock **layer** as the fossil of an ancient reptile, the creatures may have lived at the same time.

AMMONITE

Trilobites and another sea creature known as a graptolite are also used as index fossils.

BIG FINDS

Scientists are still finding the fossils of new sea creatures. Some big finds are even made by everyday people! In 2020, a giant pliosaur skull was found in a cliff in Dorset, England.

That same year, a father and daughter found the **jaw** of a bigger sea creature while walking on a beach in Somerset, England. This creature was found to be a kind of ichthyosaur.

FUN FACT

THE ICHTHYOSAUR FOUND IN SOMERSET MAY HAVE BEEN OVER 82 FEET (25 M) IN LIFE.

Ichthyosaurs may look
like dolphins, but they're
not related at all!

FINDING SEA CREATURE FOSSILS

While a good place to find sea creature fossils is on the beach, it's not the only place to find them! Sea creature fossils can be found nearly anywhere. Some fossils have even been found on the tops of mountains! This is because these areas used to be under the ocean.

To see fossils up close, you can also visit a **museum**. The Natural History Museum of Los Angeles County has many marine fossils for visitors to see.

How Fossils Form

An ammonite lives on ancient Earth.

When the ammonite dies, it falls to the seafloor. Over time, it is buried by sediment.

The ammonite's soft body breaks down. Only its shell is left behind.

The shell is preserved as a fossil over millions of years.

GLOSSARY

abundant: Something found in large amounts.

arthropod: An animal that lacks a backbone and has a skeleton on the outside of its body, such as an insect, spider, shrimp, or crab.

detail: One small part.

environment: The natural world in which a plant or animal lives.

extinct: No longer living.

jaw: One of the two bones of the face where teeth grow.

layer: One thickness of something lying over or under another.

museum: A building in which things of interest are displayed.

permineralization: A process of fossilization in which a mixture of water and minerals flow into a dead organism and fill its empty spaces.

pressure: A force that pushes on something else.

sediment: Matter, such as stones and sand, that is carried onto land or into the water by wind, water, or land movement.

skeleton: The strong frame that supports an animal's body.

FOR MORE INFORMATION

Books

Drimmer, Stephanie Warren. *Prehistoric Sea Monsters.* Washington, DC: National Geographic, 2024.

Secher, Andy. *Travels with Trilobites: Adventures in the Paleozoic.* New York, NY: Columbia University Press, 2022.

Websites

Britannica Kids: Fossils
https://kids.britannica.com/kids/article/fossil/353144
Learn more about the different types of fossils found in the world.

Penn Dixie
https://penndixie.org/
Plan a visit to dig your own trilobite fossils at Penn Dixie Fossil Park & Nature Reserve.

INDEX